TEACH YOUR
BUILD A POSITIVE SELF
IMAGE

RAISE CONFIDENT, RESILIENT
AND HAPPY CHILDREN

Written by ELA SENGHERA

Foreword by Dr. ANDY WIENER

Dedication

This book is dedicated to all parents around the world.

May you find balance, joy, and happiness in doing the most important job out there - raising children. I hope you build a beautiful, life-long relationship with your kids. One that is based on trust, love, and mutual respect.

CONTENTS

INTRODUCTION

While most parents are aware of children's physical growth, the bond with their child also plays a huge role in their brain development. By the age of five, a child's brain is 90% developed and so are most of their beliefs about the world and people around them. The emotional development of children largely depends on loving relationships with responsible adults present in a child's life. Children's relationships with adults are the key to a healthy life as they set the foundation of their emotional maturing. During early years, children learn how to experience emotions, express them, and relate to others.

Another factor that has a big impact on children's future is how a child sees and relates to themselves on a daily basis. Their self-image and self-esteem start forming from an early age and have a big impact on how a child's future will play out. How a child sees themselves affects their everyday life. When they accept themselves for who they are, they are likely to identify their strengths and positive aspects of their character, and therefore more likely to excel at school, work, and in their social life. However, these days many children will grow up in families where high stress levels are present or they might be raised by a parent who might have a mild form of a mental illness.

When parents have access to support, they can minimize the impact their current circumstances have on their children. However, when this support is missing, things can look very different, especially when a child has a poor self-image. When faced with adverse events, all children and adults develop various coping mechanisms. Some of them are healthy and some of them can be considered unhealthy. Regardless of this, both children and adults are always in the company of their own thoughts, their inner voice, and their self-esteem, which is present in whatever they do. Helping your child develop a positive self-image and a good level of self-esteem is as important as giving them hugs, kisses, and sending them to the best school. There are many ways in which you can support your child's mental well-being and help them thrive. One of the best ways to ensure mental well-being in children is crucial to provide them with a consistent family life where they feel safe and supported by their parents. This family life should be one where building a positive self-image is encouraged and promoted by responsible adults. Parenthood is not easy at the best of times. All families face challenges but you deal with them means everything. Challenges in families don't necessarily mean that the emotional development of children will suffer. Parents can often feel overwhelmed and stressed out and can struggle with staying balanced and calm. I have created this book to empower you with knowledge and skills and support you in building a positive self-image in your child. Positive self-image is something that is not often discussed, but it's a crucial part of developing a positive mental health, strong resilience, and true-life skills in our children. Poor self-image can cause future emotional, physical, and behavioral problems in our kids. We, parents, can change that. Treat this book as a simple guide in understanding common issues adolescent children face and unravel some complexities of their emotions.

Among other things in this book, we will discuss:

- *What are the signs of low self-esteem in our children?*
- *How to identify limiting beliefs and change them into supportive ones*
- *How to spot negative thinking patterns and challenge them*
- *How do peers and friends influence how our children see themselves?*
- *What is an inner voice and how to help your child develop one?*

- *How to help develop confidence and self-acceptance in your child*
- *How to cultivate self-discipline and create healthy habits in our children*

FOREWORD

by Dr. Andy Wiener

In my work as a consultant child and adolescent psychiatrist at a renowned therapy center, the Tavistock Clinic, I often see children and young people who, for a complex set of reasons, have been unable to cope with challenges and upheavals that life has put in their way.

However, it is well recognised that children who are resilient do better in life. They are able to better cope with life challenges and bounce back faster following difficult life events. Resilient children may, with any luck, not have to see someone like me! Although, good quality parenting is not the complete answer for building childhood resilience, it certainly is a major contributor. ''Teach Your Kids to Build a Positive Self-Image'' is a practical guide for parents on how to build confidence and resilience in children of any age. In her book, Ela comes to this task with humility. She knows from firsthand experience that being a parent is not easy.

Although having a child can bring joy beyond all bounds, parenthood can also be a major challenge. There are many parents who can benefit from the advice included in this book. However, the key is to start putting these ideas into practice long before things start to go wrong. Readers of the book should be reassured that the author has a real lived experience of parenthood and that the concepts covered throughout this book are well established and evidence based. Ela's approach to parents supporting their children is based on Cognitive Behavioral Therapy (CBT) and Neuro-Linguistic Programming (NLP). Both are well recognised approaches to improving mental health in children and adults.

''Teach Your Kids to Build a Positive Self Image'' is a good reminder that whatever happens, parents need to put their children first. Parents need to focus on treating their children with sensitivity, openness, and compassion, alongside practical support, and a positive motivational stance with structure and discipline. This approach really does give children the best start in life and helps them develop coping skills necessary to face the ups and downs of life.

I welcome Ela's book which is a good guide to helping parents build resilience in their children and therefore helps them achieve their full potential.

<u>1</u>

WHAT IS SELF-ESTEEM?

Self-esteem is your internal picture. It often describes how you see yourself in your day-to-day life. It's often based on opinions that we have of ourselves and it really largely is shaped by our environment. This is why it's difficult for us to convince people to change this perception. You need to be first aware of what your self-esteem is before you can try changing it. There are different factors that determine how we see ourselves. Some of these factors might be our childhood, our family or friends, our past experiences, and where we live. However, regardless of all these, we should always work on having a healthy level of self-esteem.

Self-esteem can be a little hard to understand at times, but it really is one of the key factors that determine the state of our and our children's mental health. Our self-esteem can determine if we are likely to excel at certain tasks and explore our full potential. It really affects our decision-making skills and it's one of the key factors that can determine how our future will play out.

For example, someone who really loves sports but has a low self-esteem is likely to underestimate his potential at sports and is very unlikely to practice long and hard enough to become a football player compared to someone who might have a vague interest in sports but practices regularly and really enjoys it and makes slow but steady progress. Self-esteem is really important to understand. It really affects our decision-making skills. Having the right knowledge on self-esteem and positive self-image might change our perception of who we are and what our lives are about, and it can greatly improve the course of our future. Let's talk about how self-esteem affects us. When your child has low self-esteem, you might not see it straight away. You might see them as a little introverted or quiet, but you need to be careful of assumptions like that. Generally, a child that has a low self-esteem will try to avoid various situations. They may try different tricks to avoid situations where they could get stressed out or anxious, where they have to speak in public, or any sort of situation where they could get stressed out or embarrassed.

So, a child with a low self-esteem could:

- *Avoid tasks or challenges*
- *They could give up easily without trying hard enough*
- *They could avoid making new friends or social situations*
- *They could be quiet and withdrawn*
- *They could try avoid going to school*
- *Avoid situations where they need to be social and engaging because they are not confident*

Also, your child might start to perform badly at school, or they might become obsessed with gaining approval from others like their peers and friends. They may try really hard to impress their peers because their inner confidence and self-image is not good enough. So, your child might really start relying on the approval of others. Your child may also lose interest in activities that they would normally enjoy and they might end up spending lots of time by themselves. These behaviors can change your perception of your child. You need to be aware of these changes because it might be that only when you are close to your child and when you observe them, you might notice it, otherwise it can go unnoticed. All of these behaviors can impact your child in a negative way in the long term. Having a low self-esteem might really take a toll on how much they enjoy life, how much they explore, and how much they engage with others. And it could also affect how you feel about your family.

2

CLOSE RELATIVES OF LOW SELF-ESTEEM

Let's now move on and talk about other issues that are connected to low self-esteem. These issues might often go unnoticed but in many cases, they are present when your child has low self-esteem. They might be the direct reason for the poor self-image and low level of confidence in your child. The most common relatives of low self-esteem are bullying, exam stress, anxiety, and depression.

BULLYING

Bullying is an aggressive unwanted behavior which is usually very harmful, intimidating, or offensive. It has a purpose to insult, or damage reputation, or embarrass the victim. Bullying is a behavior that is often repeated or has the potential to be repeated over time. Both the bully and the victim are suffering from serious long-term effects. Kids who bully others usually use their power such as physical strength, embarrassing information, or their popularity to threaten or intimidate others. Bullies often need help too as they often try to make themselves feel big by making other children feel small. So as difficult as it is to accept the damaging behavior they are causing, it's worth remembering that they are often the ones who need help themselves. Bullies usually feel small or worthless, so by making others feel small and worthless they feel powerful and good, but underneath they are still the same. Bullies use their power to embarrass others. And power imbalances can change over time and, of course, in different situations, even if they involve the same people. However, bullying can be difficult to notice or acknowledge, especially to a child that has a low self-esteem. There could be mixed messages, it could be confusing to understand. Oftentimes bullying starts with a small comment, sometimes not threatening in its nature. It can manifest itself as a small comment that is repeated on a regular basis, with a purpose to hurt someone.

CYBERBULLYING

Cyberbullying is when bullying happens online. It can happen through an SMS, messaging app, or a social media or gaming platform. And it usually has the purpose to embarrass or belittle the victim and make them feel low and miserable. Cyberbullying is also manifesting itself via sending, sharing, or posting embarrassing information or embarrassing images. If a child has a healthy level of self-esteem that was created in their childhood, such a child when exposed to bullying is going to care far less about being bullied then someone who has a low self-esteem. Of course, a child with a healthy level of self-esteem will still find it extremely disturbing that someone is being mean to them or is calling them names but is more likely to actually look at that individual with a little bit of empathy and almost lack of understanding why would they be doing this, thinking "there's *nothing wrong with me*". This happens because this child has formed a healthy attachment to both or one of the parents and is usually trusting that parent. It would be the same parent who has played a crucial role in helping their child build a healthy level of self-image. This parent is likely to find out that something is going wrong in their child's life.

EXAM STRESS

Exam stress is something very common but it can have a really big impact on children's lives. Oftentimes it affects children and adolescents during exam time. While a small amount of stress can be helpful to keep kids motivated and really focused, a larger level of stress that persists longer can be really damaging to them. When kids don't know how to deal with stress it can really affect their sleep, their diets, and their general well-being. It's therefore very important that we, parents, know how to help our children during exam time, to make their life a little bit easier, and to teach them how to cope during this difficult time. So it's essential for us to help them look after themselves and support their well-being, and not give into stress and pressure. Do you know how to recognise that your child is struggling with exam stress? What are the typical symptoms that are the red flags that we should be aware of?

Some of the symptoms can include:

- *feeling moody or low*
- *feeling easily overwhelmed*
- *having low energy levels*
- *having trouble making decisions*
- *losing touch with friends*
- *lack of interest in activities they usually enjoy*
- *losing appetite or overeating*
- *having problems with falling asleep or waking up at night*
- *having problems getting out of bed in the morning*

- *difficulty getting motivated to get back to studying*
- *biting nails*
- *experiencing headaches or tummy aches*

If this is something you hear on a daily basis from your child, it might mean you need to be more proactive in teaching your child how to manage stress. Feeling a little nervous during exam time is completely different. But if you notice the above symptoms in your child over a few days or weeks as a parent, you really need to be more proactive. Do you know what to do to help ease stress? There are few things you can do. You could start with the following:

- *start with helping them get things ready the night before*
- *make sure they eat healthy breakfast before they leave the house*
- *drop them off or remind them how to get there*
- *talk to them about what it means to them if they don't get the desired outcome from their exams?*

Children need to understand that no matter what results they get; it's not the end of the world and you are not going to stop loving them. They should not think of themselves as any less than they are, just because they didn't get the grades they were hoping for. Also, creating an environment where they can switch off and unwind after school and in the evenings can be very helpful.

Some other ideas to ease off the exam stress are:

- *Going for nature walks or playing outside*
- *Switching off mobiles before going to sleep at least an hour before*
- *Limiting screen time*
- *Watching funny movies with them*
- *Encouraging them to rest and relax*
- *Encouraging participating in activities that are going to give them perspective when they are not studying*
- *Asking for their help with shopping or other chores will help them gain perspective that life goes on and build resilience*

Crucial point is that children should have time away from the screen. They should not be obsessed with constantly being online or communicating with their friends. If they are, you need to set some boundaries. Kids need to learn from us, so try to model positive behavior. They need to allow themselves time and space to breathe, relax, go for walks, or play football. Simple daily exercises can really help. Perhaps you can organize a family meal out or take them shopping when they are not studying. This might really help.

SOCIAL ANXIETY

Social anxiety is very common. It's a spectrum and it becomes a disorder if there is significant impairment (for example: low school attendance or social isolation). It affects children's confidence, their self-esteem. and self-image. It affects their life by reducing the number of activities they get involved in and has a huge negative impact on their friendships. Children with social anxiety can get very anxious about going to shops, restaurants, and to school. Social anxiety can really cloud their thinking and make them overthink small details. Despite the fact that social anxiety is very common we don't often talk about it and most parents aren't aware of it, but it's really worth knowing that social anxiety can lead to social anxiety disorder which is a mental health condition that can have a huge negative impact on your child. Because of the sensitive brain development period and the need to build their own identity, children really crave contact with peers. Without it they can suffer from low self- confidence, poor social skills, and are unable to focus on studying and enjoying life.

Having social anxiety makes day-to-day activities very hard. Especially if this involves activities in a school, class presentation, or just talking to people. Social anxiety is often connected to low confidence and poor self-esteem. This is because the core beliefs of kids who have a social anxiety disorder is that they are not good enough. They see themselves through a clouded view and it makes them believe that they are not capable of doing things other people can do. These thoughts translate deeper into their core beliefs system, which can be hard to change. This is why it's important to spot the signs of social anxiety early.

There are few things you can do to help your child:

1. **Educate them.** Explain that it's normal to feel anxious from time to time and they should not allow their fears to stop them from enjoying life. Help them understand what it is they are afraid of and what is the worst-case scenario that can happen? How will that really affect them?

2. **Be compassionate.** Explain that you understand it must be hard for them and that you are there for them to help them get better. Do not judge them or criticize them. Make them feel that they can always trust you and can come to you whenever they need to talk.

3. **Encourage them.** Challenge their anxious thinking and encourage them to focus on their goals. Let them tell you how great it will feel when they achieve their goals. What feelings will they experience? Explain that anxiety is not part of them and it's something they can totally learn to manage.

4. **Seek professional help.** If you do all of the above and your child is not getting better, is refusing to go out, or is becoming more anxious and isolated, it might be worth it to start seeking help. Start by speaking to a clinical psychologist. A clinical psychologist will do a generic assessment first and then recommend a treatment. Clinical psychologists are usually quite well up on the evidence base.

Take note that some child therapists, like psychotherapists and counselors in particular, will suggest an individual therapy for a child when that isn't the evidence-based treatment for the presenting problem. So be careful who you consult on this. Depending on the age of your child, a family therapy might be a much better solution than individual therapy. Individual therapy is usually much more effective for secondary school children who can benefit from it from the age of around 14 or so. Help might be also available via your GP, some charities, or a service dedicated to families via a local government. It's worth pointing out that if you feel that your child has higher than average needs, then you need to adapt your parenting style and your skills to meet their needs.

DEPRESSION

Low mood and low self-esteem often go together. When low mood persists or gets more severe it can lead to depression, and that's when you need to seek help. Sadly, depression is becoming more and more common among young people so we, parents, need to be aware of the first symptoms of depression. You might be familiar with some of the symptoms already, but let's mention them to refresh your knowledge. They are:

- *feeling low for a long period of time*
- *feeling constantly tired and low on energy*
- *poor or no sleep*
- *struggling to fall asleep*
- *inability to get out of bed*
- *changes in eating habits (for example, no eating or overeating)*
- *feeling restless or easily irritable*
- *getting easily upset or argumentative*

- *overwhelming feelings of worthlessness and guilt*
- *inability to think clearly or make decisions*
- *feeling a lack of purpose*
- *suicidal thoughts*
- *no interest in activities that normally bring joy*

Have you seen any of these signs in your child? Do any of these other issues run in your family? If you notice them in your child, it's worth speaking to your child about how they have been feeling recently and trying to get an idea what could be the root cause of the problem. Sometimes, however, there isn't a root cause, or it might be related to your mental health. Parents experiencing depression, anxiety, burnout, divorce, or separation can have a huge negative impact on a child's feelings. It's worth bearing that in mind. When you see that things are getting more serious or there is no improvement, you should seriously consider speaking to your GP or seeing a Child Psychotherapist as soon as possible. Make sure you keep a close eye on your child until things get better.

It's completely normal when your child is feeling depressed, that it has a negative impact on you and your whole family. The most important thing for you to do as a parent is to stay close to your child and understand what is the reason they are feeling like this and how long it's been going on. Going to the root cause of the problem can really help you solve or reduce the impact depression has on your child and your whole family. Depression is something that is very serious. Once you notice that your child has been feeling low for a long period of time or they have been saying that they are feeling depressed, you need to get them professional help. However, before you do that, there are few simple things you can do to improve the situation:

Talk to Your Child

Make sure your tone is non-judgmental, friendly and loving. Let your child talk and don't talk over them. It might be very difficult for your child to open up and be honest with you so show them patience and respect. Let them say everything that's on their mind so you understand their point of view. Be extra aware that you should not be making comments that are judgmental or criticizing during this conversation. Have patience and allow time and the right space for your child to really open up and tell you what's bothering them. Perhaps there was a period of intense arguments with your partner, a house move, a divorce or separation, or a change of school. All these can have a big impact on your child.

Usually, depression is about something that has been lost, so thinking with the child about what they think they might have lost could be a good angle. They might have had a physical illness so have lost fitness or mobility. They might have lost a close relative or they miss their absent father. They might be adjusting to a move to a new area or when they don't have friends. Once you know the root cause you might want to try and find remedy by doing something to make it easier for them. Say there is loss of contact with a father after a divorce. Then what you do is you could improve the quality of that contact. Say they are struggling to adjust to a house move to a new area. Then promote contact with old friends and see what opportunities are there to help your child make new friends.

Also, remember that some children are depressed because their parents, often their mother, is emotionally absent, unavailable, or is subject to substance misuse. If that is your case, then of course the solution is for you as a parent to get out of a bad relationship, out of a bad habit, and sort out your own problems first before your child can get better. Children's wellbeing often reflects the state of your own well-being. Things that cause child depression may be things that affect the whole family, for example, a bereavement. So rather than assuming that when you seek help, you seek help for your child, a better approach might be to have some family therapy so that the communication in the family can be improved and your child feels better understood. Always try to have a general assessment first that takes into account all factors impacting on a child or young person's wellbeing before recommending individual therapy for a child. If the problem is in the family, the solution is usually in the family.

Make regular time for you and your child

Dedicate some time to your child, even if it's just 15-20 minutes a day. They need to know that you are there for them and you are going to go through this process together. Really prioritize this. It doesn't matter if you have got something going on in your professional or personal life. This is your child, and they need you. Make them feel that they can trust you and rely on you. This will help them open up and find courage to deal with bigger issues that might be bothering them.

Spend time outdoors

Make sure your child gets regular time outdoors. The worst thing you can do is to allow them to stay at home in their room and, worse still, in front of a computer or smartphone. Contact with nature has been proved to play an essential role in improving well-being in children and adults. Make sure your child gets a regular time out: go for a walk with a dog, go to a park, or play football. All these can make a massive difference to your child's wellbeing.

Research and find professional help before it's too late

Make sure you dedicate enough time into researching, finding, and screening the right professional expert for that. Don't think that the first person you are going to find is going to solve all your children's problems. Depending whether you use the public or private resources, finding and booking time with a good psychotherapist can take time. Once you find them, it can be a bit like finding your match in a relationship context. Not every child therapist will have the right approach or skills to really connect with your child and help them get better. A good professional needs to be able to build trust in your child and show them compassion. So make sure you dedicate enough time to finding and researching the right person.

If you are going the private route, meet a child therapist before your child meets them

Speak with a child therapist or counselor before your child meets them. Voice your concerns and explain what you think the problem is. Make sure you dedicate enough time to this process, understand their background, and the areas of their expertise. This will give you confidence that they will be able to help your child. Don't be shy and ask for help.

Also, ask to be kept up to date about your child's progress and any feedback related to that. Ask what you can do to play your role in their recovery. It's important you have confidence in this person, so speak to them and try to understand how they work. Once your child meets them regularly, try to establish if they are getting better and if their depression is getting under control. Ask the therapist if there is anything you can do to speed up the recovery process.

There are few other things you can do to help your child when they are displaying first signs of low mood or depression. First and foremost, allow them space for self-expression. They might not be saying a lot, but they are certainly thinking a lot. All of their thoughts need to be released from their mind, otherwise they can build up in their body and cause anxiety, muscle tension, headaches, and more. So it's crucial that your child has a space to be themselves especially at home and release any negative feelings and thoughts.

Some of the things you can is to encourage them to:

- ***Keeping a journal and writing down anything that's on their mind.*** *The best results come when this is something that is used regularly. So, try to encourage, as much as possible, for them to express* *any fears or worries on a piece of paper on a regular basis. This journal will be a platform to release any negative thoughts and any anxiety. Bear in mind that self-expression is something children do through music, playing, drawing, painting, or dancing. So, get your child to make music, sing, or dance as often as possible, especially if this is something they normally enjoy doing. This might be a platform to release this trauma that they are experiencing at the moment.*

- *Do physical exercise and get moving. Physical exercise causes the body to produce endorphins, which is happiness hormones. This is what helps them in becoming happier. Sitting in their room behind closed doors is not a good solution, so always pay attention to how much time your child spends outdoors and what activities they get involved in.*

- *Get involved in volunteering, community work projects, and helping others no matter how big or small these activities are. Helping others gives both adults and children a real sense of purpose and seeing the effects of their work can be very satisfying. This can shift their mood and make them see a different perspective. Helping others makes us feel needed, which is the opposite feeling that depression creates in us.*

Here are some tips that will further help your child in preventing depression:

- *Limit screen time. Gadgets and social media are altering children's view of reality. The more screen time they have, the more time they scroll through social media, and the more they believe that perfection is real and should be the norm. This cannot be the case. That is why ensuring that they are spending more time in the real physical world is healthy for their mental health.*

- *Prioritize a nutritious diet instead of fast food. Ensuring that your child is eating healthy foods makes them stronger physically and mentally. This will ultimately boost their immune system and brain power to fight all sorts of illnesses. Fruits, vegetables are much better for their mental health than food served by the popular fast-food chains. Nutritious diet full of vitamins improves memory which is essential during exam time.*

- *Ensure that they are having fun. They are kids and they are supposed to play. Don't pressurize them too much with school and allow them to breathe, relax, and enjoy their childhood and young years. This might be hard to do during exam time, but essentially, they need time away from books or their computer.*

- ***Be a listener.*** *Always let them know that you are ready to listen to their thoughts without judgment or offering them advice.*

- ***Be their ally and offer any help that you can****. Try to build a relationship where they do most of the talking and you do more listening rather than the other way around. Make sure they know you love them, and that you will love them no matter what grades they get. Please note that this is much more achievable when you are in a good place mentally yourself, so don't forget about self-care.*

WHEN TO GET PROFESSIONAL HELP?

When your child is feeling depressed it's really important to know when and what type of help to get. As a parent you will probably know. There is nothing embarrassing about getting help. It's much worse to wait too long and do nothing. Having a depressed child can be very hard on you and your mental health, too. A professional can really help you and you don't need to do it all alone. If you are feeling overwhelmed, they can help you navigate through parenting and give you skills and strategies that bring much needed support to you and your family. If your child is feeling really sad and hopeless all the time, find and meet a child therapist as soon as possible. Arrange a meeting with them to better understand how they will be able to help. Don't wait too long as depression doesn't get better on its own. Also, if your child is not being themselves, they refuse to go to school, their grades are failing, if they struggle at school, or are self-harming or talking about self- harming, get a therapist as soon as possible. You might choose to see your GP first to get a general assessment and be directed to a specialist later on. When your child is asking to see someone, you should honor that, and get them the help they need as soon as possible. Remember that sometimes talking to someone other than your parents can be very liberating for your child. As a parent you should not get offended because of this. Sometimes we are too close to notice some issues in our children and a third person might really help identify them.

3

AUTOMATIC THOUGHTS & UNHELPFUL BELIEFS

Automatic thoughts are a short stream of thoughts that we have about ourselves or others. They usually happen quite quickly and can be triggered by an event, for example, a school exam. They can become more intense when a child is anxious, tired, or depressed. Most of the time children and adults are not aware of their automatic thoughts. However, we quickly become familiar with the feelings they cause. In the case of a school exam most kids' automatic thoughts would be a feeling of fear or a slight anxiety. For us, parents, identifying these automatic thoughts in our kids is an important step to help them in creating a positive view of the world. This is because our kids' view of the world consists of many different smaller thoughts related to different people, events, or things.

Automatic thoughts often have the following characteristics:

- *They appear as just one word or a short phrase and function as a label for a group of memories or group of fears. However, they don't always appear as words. They can be stored in our mind as a visual image, a sound, smell, or a physical sensation*
- *They are almost always believed, no matter how illogical they may seem*
- *They are experienced as spontaneous and automatic, meaning that we don't realize when they appear.*

To make this a bit simpler for you, let's give an example. A child is having an exam and the first automatic thought a nervous child might think is *"fail"*. It might be that this thought is so strong that it happens every time the idea of the exam appears. The most important message to give to your child is thoughts cause feelings. The emotions that we feel are always caused by their thoughts. So, the thought comes first, the feeling comes second. The second most important thing we need to remember is that events in themselves do not contain feelings or emotions. An event is just something that happens. It's only our interpretation of the event that causes us to feel different emotions.

Automatic thoughts tend to make the situations worse, feel worse, seem more negative, and even sometimes make it look or feel really catastrophic. So, they catastrophize and stir the reality around us. Automatic thoughts are learned and can be totally unlearned. It just takes some practice. They create a tunnel vision approach to different situations so we fall into a certain pattern of thinking once we start with an automatic thought that leads to another one because that leads to a feeling and then it can lead to a prediction or a mind reading where we envisage the future in a certain way, which can be very far from the truth.

It's important that we teach our children that we all have automatic thoughts and that we interpret our experiences every day through our senses: what you see, what you hear, and what you feel or touch. We judge these things as good or bad, happy or sad, upsetting or enjoyable, or perhaps safe or risky. So, we make judgments in our mind every single day. Those judgements, and how we categorize a specific event, very often starts from an automatic thought. You can see how difficult it is to change that pattern of thinking, because if we don't realize that we have a certain automatic thought related to an event, it's not going to be that easy to change the end result of that thought. Most of the time we don't notice our thoughts, but they can be so powerful that they can create very intense feelings and emotions inside our bodies. So, when a child is feeling low or anxious, it's very important to tell them about those automatic thoughts and the fact that we all have them. It's about practicing the ability of spotting those automatic thoughts before they become more serious and before we or our children fall into the pattern of a negative spiral. Let's spot them early and let's try to interpret them in a different way. The more we practice, the better we are going to become at it. The more we encourage our children to notice those automatic negative thoughts, the more aware they are going to be of them in the future. And this is the first step. It just takes practice. It's totally possible to change and unlearn your automatic thoughts. It's this ability to interpret the thoughts that will define whether your child will not get affected too much by a specific event or a situation or if your child will gradually start seeing the world in a very negative way and at some point, might need professional help.

CHALLENGING UNHELPFUL BELIEFS

Now let's move on and talk about challenging unhelpful beliefs. What is a belief? A belief is the thought that we keep thinking. It's a thought that we regularly think. Our beliefs can support us in achieving our goals or they can work against us. Both children and adults have different beliefs that were formed based on our past experiences and thoughts related to those past experiences. As we spoke earlier, our thoughts cause different feelings. It's not an event that makes us feel in a certain way but it's the interpretation of that event.

Our thoughts can make us happy, sad, lonely, misunderstood, angry, disappointed, and so on. This is because of something that happened to us before, which was when the beliefs were formed. If an event occurs and it causes us to have a certain thought, that thought causes us a specific feeling. And those feelings are stored in our minds and make us associate a specific event or a situation with a specific feeling. For example, a child might have a school exam - that's the event. And they may associate that event with the feeling of fear or a tummy ache. Those feelings, or thoughts to start with and feelings later, all get stored in our subconscious mind. So what our children think and tell themselves determines the level of self-esteem. It also affects their confidence and their future life choices. This is why it's so important for us parents to promote positive self-dialogue in our children and teach them how to control their negative thinking. There are few ways in which we can decrease negative thought patterns in our children. For example, if a child is refusing to take part in a public speaking event because they think they're not good enough, we could challenge them and try to ask them different questions. For example, we could change the auditory experience. So ask your child to picture themselves standing in front of their classmates. What voices do they hear? Chances are they are thinking of a nervous voice, one that is criticizing them. Suggest to them to switch the voice in their mind to something funny. For example, instead of hearing voices of their peers that they are criticizing, laughing, or being negative, let's ask the child to imagine that their friends or classmates have voices of cartoon characters. That immediately changes, in our child's mind, this situation into a less serious one and gives them an opportunity to reconsider speaking in public because it suddenly doesn't feel like it's such a big deal.

Another great way to transform negative self-talk into positive internal dialogue is to challenge the lack of confidence and by asking questions that give you more information.

For example, in the event of public speaking we could ask them:

- *How do you feel about the event?*
- *What causes you to feel that way?*
- *When do you usually feel like that?*
- *When do you not feel like that?*
- *How would you prefer to feel instead, in a situation like this?*

Once you have more information, we can ask questions that challenge the feelings or unwillingness to participate in an event. This way we can change a limiting belief. For example, a belief that a child is not good enough to speak in public. It might be that they are not even able to voice this clearly or be aware that this is a belief. But it might be that this has been on their mind for a long time, and it might have limited how they enjoy life. A limiting belief is a mindset or thought pattern that a child believes to be their reality. Beliefs rule a person's behaviors and what follows afterwards - so the results of their behavior. If your child shows lack of confidence based on limiting beliefs, you can understand them better by observing their behavior and asking questions, like the ones we have mentioned before. Another way to help your child boost their confidence is to convert from present to past. For example, if your child says a statement such as, *"I can't finish my homework"*, ask them to say, *"in the past, I couldn't finish my homework, but now it happens so quickly"*. You can say similar statements in the past tense and that will help boost your child's self-esteem.

Another way of challenging limiting beliefs is to use **Future Imagery**.

If you find your child is stuck in an endless cycle of low self-esteem, ask them to imagine a scenario in the future where they are doing all those things that they aren't able to now (for example, dancing on the stage or performing in front of many people). Imagining those things will give them courage. Once children visualize themselves in those situations that cause them anxiety in normal circumstances, the more they practice those visualizations - the more courage they will actually get to perform this task in real life.

You can also use affirmations to make the impact of future visualization even more powerful.

<u>4</u>

HELP YOUR KIDS BATTLE NEGATIVE THINKING

As some of you might know, negative thinking is one of the main reasons for having low self-esteem. Negative thinking really is the root of the majority of mental stress and that affects both us and our children. So, when battling negative thinking, one of the most common things people usually do is just distract themselves. When they're feeling stressed or worried, they distract themselves with a different activity. The truth is that distraction only works for a short period of time. So, to really effectively control your negative thinking, you need to face it. The same applies to children. Children need to acknowledge that they have negative thoughts first before they can start turning them into positive thoughts. There are three key steps you can take to help your child fight negative thoughts.

1. *Identify them*
2. *Fight them with positive thoughts*
3. *Stop negative thinking from becoming a real negative spiral*

Step one is that you have correctly identified negative thoughts and ideally the sooner, the better. So ideally you want to strive towards teaching your child to catch when they're having automatic negative thoughts and recognise it. Of course, we may not, most of the time, be aware of our thoughts but it's really important for both children and adults to build a habit of recognising when negative thinking is really getting out of control. That usually starts from very small thoughts about a person or event or a scary situation or an uncomfortable situation. Something we don't want to do, something we don't like. Teaching your child how to spot when the first thought like that appears in their head is already 50% of the success. Once we teach our children how to identify them, we can move to the next step, which is to fight them with positive thoughts. As we know, negative thoughts are the thoughts that feed low self-esteem. They can really make us feel disempowered, frustrated, or weak. They make our children feel like they're not capable of things, they will never be successful, they're not good enough. They can make our kids feel like it's not worth trying something new, because the result is going to be embarrassing. So, they can really disempower our children. On the other hand, positive thoughts give us hope, strength, and confidence. So positive thoughts often tell us indirectly about our abilities and our unique qualities and explaining that to our children is very important. It's important to explain the difference between positive thoughts and negative thoughts and teaching our kids to spot that difference is the real key to success. Whenever we identify a negative thought, we should neutralize it with a positive thought.

So, whenever your child is having a negative thought, tell them to fight it with a positive thought coming to their head that might help to neutralize the situation. So, what does this mean? It means that they will be able to switch from a disempowered thinking and disempowered mindset into the type of thinking and mindset that allows them to flourish. Show your child a difference between a negative thought and a positive one. Give them examples of how to create a positive thought. For example, when a child is going to have an exam their first thought might be that I will fail. The idea is that we help our child identify this thought as negative and not a fact, not as a reality, because it isn't a reality.

So, what we would like to say to them to help them find a positive thought could be something like *"if I prepare myself enough, the results could be good"* or *"If I prepare myself this week, everything will go well"*. As you can see this thought is not super positive or ecstatic but it's a positive one. From *"I will fail"* to *"If I prepare myself, everything will go well"*, there is a big difference in mindset here. And that's the idea! To shift your mindset from negative to positive so that negative thinking doesn't limit your or your children's lives and taking part in activities that are good for their health and development. Just take a note, though, that whenever you tell your child to fight a negative thought with a positive one, they are probably not going to listen to you to start with.

They may not believe you because they think that you don't know them or you don't know the reality of how hard it is. So just take a note that you should not be telling your child what they should be thinking or what they should be saying to themselves. You are simply just guiding them through the process of how to turn a negative thought into a positive one and showing them the benefit of that. It is their choice how they word those sentences and how they really form those positive thoughts.

Your role is to guide them and teach them and show them how this can be done. Your child needs to learn how to generate positive thoughts without your help. This is something that will help them for the rest of their lives. It's a skill that will be extremely valuable for the rest of their lives. So, it's really important that you as a parent encourage your child with patience and with understanding on how to take control and turn them into a positive, impactful behavior. This is step number one. Step number two is identify negative thoughts and fight them with positive thoughts.

Number three is crush *"snowball thinking"*. Snowball thinking happens when negative thought is becoming stronger and stronger, and you could say it fights back. So just like a snowball, when it goes down the hill and picks up more snow, more speed, and more power, and it catches momentum, the further down the hill it goes, in the same way our thoughts become stronger, more powerful, and more negative. And sometimes they will fight back.

Your mind chatter and your child's mind chatter will try to control you. When it fights back it becomes stronger and this is completely normal. It happens to everyone all the time. What you need to do is get used to fighting back with strong beliefs and perhaps slightly different positive thoughts. Sometimes you lose those battles and sometimes you win. It can go either way. But the most important thing is that you always try to fight back and crush these negative thoughts that affect you or your child. We need to tell our children that everyone has negative thoughts, it's completely normal. But fighting back those thoughts and changing them into positive ones is super important and getting them used to practicing it will really transform their lives. They will become happier, more engaged in different activities. They will have a more positive outlook on life. A good way to help them with that is to set up little challenges for them.

Challenges are a good way of helping our kids crush their worries, their anxiety, and their negative thoughts. The way it works is that when your child is negative or worried or just seems a bit down, and it happens on a regular basis, it's very likely that they have no control over their negative thinking. Most children don't and this is when anxiety really grows and develops and becomes a daily part of our life, unfortunately. So the concept of setting up challenges to encourage them to fight their worries is usually a very successful one. The idea is that you help them turn all anxiety producing situations into little challenges that they have to overcome. If they succeed, they receive a reward.

Reward is something you can talk to them about. Talk to your child about why they would like to set up those challenges. What fears are we talking about? What reward will they like to get and how will it make them feel? This will make them excited. It will motivate them to control their mind better.

How does this work in practice?

1. *Take a piece of paper and a pen and list all anxiety-producing and worry-producing situations that your child experiences. Anything that springs to mind. You can do this together with your child.*
2. *Rank all those worries from 1 to 10, with 10 being the most anxiety-provoking*
3. *List the rewards that your child will get after they complete certain activities or certain challenges.*

Take a note that not all worries are situations or activities. Some of them might be just an abstract idea. For example, they might be too afraid of a failure like in the instance of an exam. So you should think of a good activity that challenges that fear. For example, review the failed exam and challenge them to study the topics again until they become well prepared on this topic. You can make them answer the exam questions again and if they get it right - they get a reward. But you should also remember that the challenges are just a tool to help your child - so you cannot force them into doing this. You really need to get a greenlight from them and you really need to get their alignment with you on that, because if you don't - it misses the point entirely. Just to give you an example, if your child is afraid, has social anxiety, and is afraid to go to a restaurant, you could say to them: "I can order the food or you can take this challenge and you will get a reward". In this way, they will have a choice and they will feel empowered in the knowledge that they have a choice, and they are more likely to take part. And if they still choose not to take part because they're really worried and really scared, for example, then you have to acknowledge that and accept that and you need to make them feel that you have their back.

Whenever they feel like doing it or not doing it, you have their back. If you have discussed these challenges with your child and you feel like they're on board with this and they want to take part and they're showing signs that they are interested in learning how to fight negative thinking or anxiety provoking thoughts, it's great that this is something they're interested in, but it's not the end. You just need to bear in mind that there are different factors that can affect the effectiveness of this, so you need to constantly update your lists and ranking of different anxiety-provoking situations to really sustain this challenge and to really see the good results from that. It's really worth investing your time into creating a list of top worries and most common negative thoughts in your child and the biggest anxiety-provoking events and really rating them and setting up those challenges. It is something that will really help them take control over the situation. It will help your child grow and develop and become a more positive individual and, in the future, a more positive adult. However, you need to be balancing the challenges and the rewards.

Sometimes you might have the best intentions but you might be wrong in weighing the degree of the worries so you could have, for example, ranked a small fear with 8 and a huge fear with 3, because at the time it seemed like that, but the situation has changed. So, you need to keep that in mind. Our reality changes and our perception of the world changes. Our anxieties and worries can change slightly or they can shift into a different direction, so it's worth observing your child and interacting with them and having conversations about this. And notice - is that something they are really worried about the most now?

Is the old fear or old anxiety still there? Or is it something new now? Has it changed? Children change as they grow and develop and their worries and anxieties change, too.

Some of our fears are also just too big to break down and too much for a child to face. It might seem that no reward is good enough to make them take the leap. It is just something that paralyzes them. In this case, try breaking down the really big fears into smaller challenges and rank them again 1-10. We are breaking it down into smaller steps that are easier to tackle and see how your child enjoys this, what works best, see how you could help your child break their fears into smaller steps that they can cope with. Have a think about it. It's definitely something worth talking about.

5

HELP CONTROL THEIR MIND CHATTER

The power of your child's voice is huge. The most important words are the words they say to themselves when others don't listen. These words can be very positive or they can be very critical or they could be something in between. Both children and adults who have high levels of self-esteem and self-worth speak kindly to themselves. Of course, these people also have bad days so they can be a little bit critical towards themselves from time to time. But on average people with high levels of self-esteem talk kindly to themselves. People with low self-esteem see life as very black and white. For them, things are either great or they are very bad and they often compare themselves to others. So, think about what is your inner voice and what is the inner voice of your child. How do they speak to themselves? Is the voice likely to be gentle and supportive or do they mainly criticize themselves and sound really harsh when they talk about themselves? Pay attention to how your child talks about themselves, their skills, their dreams, and their goals. How does the voice sound? Do they talk about themselves in a positive light? It's really important to take control of our thoughts and our mind chatter because we are capable of much more when our voice is kind, soft, and supportive rather than strong and demanding.

Our inner voice often criticizes us. This is something that happens to everyone on this planet. Some of us are more self-critical than others but we all have this inner mind chatter and taking control over this mind chatter is really important. Did you know that when your inner voice is harsh and critical you have the same reaction as if you were arguing with someone and wanted to run away? When we are not speaking kindly to ourselves, when we are very harsh about something that we just did or something that just happened, what happens to our body at that point is that our cortisol level goes up and we don't want to do anything. We just want to run away. So this type of voice is not putting us in a frame of mind where we are motivated to do any work and improve anything. That's one interesting fact worth remembering. And that is important to bear in mind especially when it comes to our kids.

Talking kindly to our kids and really encouraging them to build this positive inner voice is something super important.

They need to learn how to be kind to themselves, how to be their own best friend. Adults and children who have low self-esteem often think that others don't think of them in a positive light. They think that even when they have no proof of it. So, the low self-esteem and this inner critic goes very much hand-in-hand. The moment our voice becomes kinder and softer and more encouraging, our self-esteem goes up. And the same applies to our children. So always try to speak to yourself as if you were speaking to your best friend. There is a very little chance, when you speak to yourself like that, that you will become lazy or you will fail. There is a huge chance, however, that when you speak kindly to yourself, you will succeed in whatever it is that you are doing.

Remember, you are there for yourself for the rest of your life. Whether you don't feel acknowledged by others, whenever you feel undermined by others, whenever as a parent you don't feel like your efforts are being seen, when you are feeling exhausted. Remember that you, becoming your own best friend, is the most important thing. The same applies to your child because you've got yourself and they've got themselves for the rest of your lives. You are always there for yourself and you can count on yourself in every situation so you need to have your back. To help your child practice positive self-talk, ask them to write down five positive affirmations. Affirmations are short sentences that signify emotional support or encouragement. Affirmations are something we repeat either in our minds or out loud when nobody is listening.

It's important that we create a habit of using affirmations regularly and really learn to believe in them as we say them out loud as they can be very helpful in identifying where this inner critic is within us and turning this inner critic into an inner friend. So the softer and more gentle the affirmations are, the more likely that they will support us in reaching our goals and dreams. There is a really big benefit behind affirmations in turning our inner critic into an inner friend. We can use our affirmations to neutralize our reaction to a stressful event or we could soothe our feelings and determine our action or our behavior following a difficult event. For example, after having an argument with a friend, we could say to ourselves (or we could write it down):

- *Everything is under control here*
- *There is nothing serious happening here*
- *Everything always works out for me and it will work out this time, too.*
- *Relationships energize me even when they are not perfect*
- *I stay true to myself and my beliefs even if others don't like it*

And the last one could be:

- *I allow myself to speak up and have a voice.*

You can see how these short sentences, these affirmations, could be used in a scenario where we just had an argument. The same applies to our children. Help your child practice positive self-talk and ask them to write down five affirmations, something that they want to use every day, something that they really like the sound of.

The second exercise could be to write a letter addressed to yourself and write it as if you were writing to your best friend. A letter that will be full of gentle, soft tone, and kind words. Thank yourself for how well you've done and mention what else you can do to support yourself in the future in raising your self-esteem and developing this inner friend.

6

SELF-CONFIDENCE

The level of self-confidence in your children usually sets the tone for almost everything they do. When a child is confident, they can deal with different life challenges on their own. That means that when a child is confident, they can be a better learner, they can be better at handling challenges or tasks, and they can be a future strong leader. Confident children also very often excel in life. They have strong coping mechanisms and they can manage their own limiting beliefs and their negative self-talk. This is most likely something you know already, but it's worth putting emphasis on that because children who are confident are really capable of much more than children who have no confidence or a low self-esteem.

In Neuro Linguistic Programming, there is strong emphasis on the language that we use with our children on a day-to-day basis. There are certain words that can boost confidence in children and there are words that can decrease that confidence. The idea is that we use those words to encourage our children and boost their confidence and we avoid certain words that crush this confidence in our kids.

Try and use different confidence boosting techniques with a child and you will see that the results are usually pretty good. You can do that in a number of ways. You could boost confidence in children using anchors. Anchoring is something that can really help instill confidence in your children. How does it work? When a child faces some confidence issues, you can ask them to recall a time when they were last confident. Ask them to think of an event when they were able to achieve their goals. Make them think of something that happened recently when they were really able to achieve what they wanted. It might be easier if you ask them to close their eyes and embrace the feelings they felt at the time of that success. Now ask your child to choose one hand gesture, something they will remember. While doing this hand gesture ask them to embrace the feelings of confidence they felt at the time of the success. This way your child is locking in a certain hand gesture with the feeling of confidence. So next time when they are feeling insecure or low on confidence, they could bring back that confidence back by doing the same hand gesture.

You could also do the same with certain colors. You could ask your child what their favorite color is and you could anchor this color with a feeling of confidence. So, you would ask your child to remember an event when they felt confident or perhaps really proud of themselves and then you ask them to imagine their favorite color. You do this a couple of times. That's when they are locking this color with confidence. And next time when they're feeling low or anxious or insecure, they are thinking of their chosen color and that brings them the feelings of confidence, pride, and inner strength. This is just a very short version of this exercise. Another thing you could do is try using modeling for gaining confidence. This is very simple. As we know, children are like sponges. They soak in everything that they observe. So, if you want your children to be confident then you should model his behavior through your thoughts, your language, and your actions. This is how your child learns - by observing you being confident in different situations.

You could try using different words of encouragement. Whenever your child is doing something, no matter how big or small, always try to take some time and appreciate their efforts. Be mindful of the words you use and the behavior you model to your children. If you want your children to be confident, you need to show confidence in yourself. When a child asks you a question, it might be something that you have absolutely no interest in but give them time and attention. Keep in mind their perspective. It might be something they're really interested in and ignoring your child for asking questions can reprogram the subconscious mind into a fear of asking questions and it might curb their curiosity. So take them asking questions as a chance to create a bond with them and perhaps even create some anchors.

While staying humble is the best of virtues, sometimes taking credit for something you did can help your children absorb that, too. So, practice self-compassion and, by doing so, show your children that it's something they should practice, too. When you're not feeling well as a parent, when you're tired, frustrated, or you just failed at something, show that vulnerability and self-compassion to your children. Explain that they will not always win. Sometimes they will fail and that's okay. Speak to them about how to deal with failure. Also, when that situation happens, say something encouraging to yourself or them. Your child will observe that and learn from this.

Try setting realistic goals. Sometimes the way you set goals for a child determines the level of self-esteem and confidence they will gain once they complete their goal. If they find something difficult, help them break down this task (or a goal) into smaller action points. Sit together and really try to break it down. This way this task will be easier to manage. There are different advantages that can come from your child reaching their goals, the main one being a massive boost in their confidence and self-worth. Remember that any time is a good time to boost your child's confidence, as this is something that can really bring great results. So try different techniques. It's all about creating a positive routine and practicing it. This can really improve the self-image and self-worth of your child's life and how they perceive the world around them.

<u>7</u>

THE POWER OF PEERS

Peers have a big impact on our children's confidence levels. Earlier we spoke about the role parents play in building positive self-esteem from an early age. But we also need to pay attention once our children are older to whom they spend time with and how this contact with this person affects our children's vision of themselves. We need to show some interest in how our child feels about themselves after meeting with their friends. We need to pay attention to how they talk about themselves, how they see themselves, how they talk about their family, and generally the world. There is a lot of research that shows the damage inflicted in the lives of those children who have not been accepted by their peers. Today's parents are often gripped by fear of their children being excluded by their friends.

One well-known writer and a psychologist concluded that a child's self-esteem has little to do with how parents see them and everything to do with the child's status in their peer group. So peers do play a big role in the self-esteem and confidence of most children. But that wasn't always the case and it's not necessarily how it should be as self-esteem that is rooted in this peer interaction is not a healthy one for our child. And the reason I say that is because an important part of growing up for a child is to have a sense of their own value and importance. When children become teenagers, peers often replace parents as they become the ones who influence children's sense of value in themselves and others. So given the importance of this self-esteem and the supposed significance of peers when shaping it, it often seems only right for us, parents, to try anything in our power to cultivate friendships for our children and make them as likable as possible. So many parents find themselves buying the clothes, supporting the activities, and facilitating the interaction that is believed to be necessary to enable their children to win new friends and hold onto them. This only seems to be the right behavior from parents, but unfortunately, it's not something that we, parents, should put as much emphasis on as we do. The issue on self-esteem is not how good a child feels about themselves, but the independence of their self-evaluation from the judgment of others.

So, what does that mean? That means:

- *How do they value themselves when they're not being valued by others?*
- *Do they believe in themselves when their words and opinions are doubted by others?*
- *Does a child accept themselves for who they are when other children judge them?*
- *Do they have this inner confidence and do they have the inner balance and grounding that they really need to create healthy levels of confidence?*

As you can see, those questions are not related to how many friends my child has and what they think of them. These questions are:

- *How do we teach our children to value themselves when they're not being valued by others?*
- *How do we make them believe in themselves when they're doubted by others?*

These skills can only be built in a relationship with a loving adult, carer, partner, or a family member. We often see the pride in a child's eyes when they are able to figure something out by themselves, stand up for themselves, and know that they are able to handle something on their own. Their true self-esteem requires psychological maturity that can only be developed through this close, loving relationship with a significant adult. In his book, *"Hold Onto Your Kids"*, Dr Gábor Máté claims that peer-oriented children when growing up are far less likely to develop a sense of independence from the way others think of them as their self-esteem will never be rooted in a self-generated valuation. Instead, their self-esteem will be conditional to what others think or speak of them and how they treat them. Peer-oriented children, which is children who take most of their advice from their peers instead of their parents, are less likely to develop a sense of independence from the way others think of them. This is because their self-esteem is not deeply rooted in self-love and self-acceptance but is conditional to what others think and speak of them. These children grow up to build their self-esteem and identity based on external factors, such as social achievement, the size of their house, or the wealth of their parents. These are not healthy measures of a healthy self-esteem in a child. A child with genuine self-esteem does not say *"I am worthy because I can do this or that"*. Instead, they believe that they are worthy whether or not they can accomplish something.

We, parents, often want to show off the things we have. We want to boast about our achievements, often through social media. We don't really invest time in building a relationship with ourselves - understanding ourselves, becoming our own best friend, understanding our emotions, or investing time in improving the way we think of ourselves or others, and practicing new healthy habits. So often we are going to social media for the easy feel-good factor. This is not something we should be teaching our children as a main source of feeling good about themselves. We need to teach them how to build an internal relationship with themselves, instead of paying attention to what others think and speak of them. If we do that then our children will always be hungry for praise and compliments. Their self-esteem will be low. It will just be filled for a moment, but it will be empty on the inside. We need to praise our children, give them compliments. But let's remember that the more praise someone gives them, the more hungry one becomes. The more popular they become, the more popular they try to be, and so on. Only a self-esteem that is independent of these things is going to serve this child for a long term. So, let's encourage our children to build this relationship with themselves, to build their inner worth, and to feel good about themselves, no matter what others think of them. Let's encourage them to build an armor of self-love and self-encouragement that will serve them their whole life.

8

INCREASE THEIR SELF-ESTEEM

We have reached lesson eight. In previous lessons, we spoke about helping our children build a kinder inner voice and manage their mind chatter. In this lesson, we will speak about another key aspect that is essential to building healthy self-esteem. I'm talking about developing self-acceptance. Self-acceptance is the basis of a healthy self-esteem. This is the case for everyone, all children and adults across all cultures around the globe need to develop self-acceptance before they can have a really strong self-esteem. According to a famous psychologist, Albert Ellis, a high self-esteem is impossible without the presence of self-acceptance. Self-acceptance becomes much easier, achievable, once we know what we need to accept.

You might have also heard about the concept of the inner being. What is it? Well, we all have an inner being and we have a relationship with this inner being. This is our inner voice or our inner essence. Some of us call it our soul or our friend. And this inner being is neither good nor bad, it just exists. You can call it in different ways or perhaps not even be aware of it, but it's something we all have. And the same way our life changes, the same way the relationship with our inner being changes. It's always evolving. At some point, our relationship can be friendly and positive, and this is very reflective in a kind inner voice.

It might change with time because something happened. It could be different every day but the idea is that it's stable and positive. Some external factors, for example, what other people say about us and different life events can impact how our relationship with our being looks like. The fact remains that building and maintaining self-acceptance is essential to developing positive self-esteem. Once you have accepted who you are, how you are, and the things you can and can't change around you, it's much easier to accept yourself fully and that is just a few steps away from developing self-confidence. And this is why it's so critical for our kids. They need to learn how to accept themselves for who they are and how they are. At the same time, they need to acknowledge that they are separate from their thoughts and feelings. So, they are not their thoughts and they are not their feelings. That is something they experience but it's not them. It's important especially for young people to know that we all have negative thoughts and feelings no matter who we are but we can always work on that and improve it. Perhaps this is something you can speak to the children about.

Start a conversation around how you personally manage having a bad day when you experience negative feelings.

- *How do you, their parents, stay stable, not perfect at all times, but stable and balanced?*
- *How do you achieve that balance, what do you do?*
- *How do you manage your weaknesses?*

However, let's discuss how it looks in real life. For example, if your child accepts that they easily get angry, they have a chance to do something about it. If they never accept it but just ignore it, then this anger can come out and blow out when they least expect it. People who have low self-esteem have lots of frustration built up. Oftentimes they don't live their lives the way they would like. So self-acceptance is the first step towards creating the life you want. It is also often connected with self-worth.

Our self-worth is the way in which we perceive ourselves and our life. There is a general self-worth which is stable and doesn't change much. That refers to the way in which we see ourselves every day. This doesn't depend on external goods or external conditions. Our general self-worth is not related to how big our house is or how expensive our car is or who our friends are. Or in terms of our children - what is their latest game or mobile phone. So that is a general self-worth. We also have a relative self-worth which is based on the following things:

- *how we feel when somebody gives us a compliment*
- *how we feel when we buy an expensive watch*
- *how we feel when we wear cool, trendy clothes*

What we, parents, need to strive for is to build strong self-worth in our children that is not related to how many friends our children have on social media and so on. It's not always easy or straightforward to do it, but this is what we should aim for. So don't feel discouraged if you've tried building a healthy self-worth in your child but it didn't work. Some children come into the world with sensitive temperaments and seem to suffer more than others from difficulties that life throws at them. Likewise, some children seem to come into the world being able to *"survive"* adversity without it having an impact on their self-esteem. So just be determined and try your best but don't get completely discouraged if it doesn't work out.

So, you might know that our self-worth comes from our childhood and people who are around us. Ever since we are small, we hear from others how we are, who we are, and this is the same for our children. Family has a crucial impact on how children see themselves and the level of self-acceptance, self-confidence, and self-worth that is formed during childhood. However, life experiences are also very important. Low level of self-worth has a big impact on negative thoughts appearing in your child's life. Negative thinking promotes negative interpretation of the reality around us, which promotes a poor self-image. It's a vicious cycle. So we need to break the cycle and we need to work harder on building strong inner worth in our children.

We have certain mechanisms which we use to feel better. In terms of adults, we are trying to feel better about ourselves often by buying a new gift, a new watch, or some jewelry. We are trying to say, *''Hey, look at me, I'm worthy because of my beautiful car''*. It applies to us, children and adults, all of us. Your child might want to have an expensive gift, or new earrings or new sneakers. But actually, healthy self-worth has nothing to do with that. Let your child know that the financial worth of the things they possess has very little to do with their inner self - worth. With high self-esteem comes emotional freedom, which is the ability to choose how to react, how to feel, what actions to take. So what does it mean? It means that the people who have positive levels of self-esteem have emotional freedom. They don't depend on others, on their compliments, opinions, or approval to feel good. They just feel good about who they are, no matter what they have.

With this good level of self-esteem comes the freedom to live the way they want to live. And this is something really important for our children to learn. Once our kids have positive self-esteem, they will be more likely to follow their dreams, follow their goals, and take action towards their goals. So put simply, the better the child feels about themselves, the more likely they are to take responsibility for their actions and create the type of future they really desire. So not just dream but actually translate their dreams into action. What we parents need to strive towards is to help our children feel good about who they are, no matter what they have or who they're friends with. So, the compliments and criticisms they receive, especially the one coming from peers, should make a little impact on them. Of course, we all like compliments, adults like them, children like them, children probably even more. But there is a big difference between liking a compliment and appreciating it and relying on a compliment and approval to feel good about who you are.

Let's not forget that people with low levels of self-esteem are very sensitive to how others see them. So, they take loads of things to heart, it's quite easy to hurt them. They can be quite unhappy about everything and they can be obsessed with their image and what other people think of them. Those who don't like themselves are not happy about who they are, quite often wish they were different but they don't do anything to change it. They don't have that courage. They don't have that ability to translate their dreams into action. What happens is that there is a lot of internal frustration built up inside those kids.

It's really important to work on raising your child's self-esteem as it builds resilience. This resilience is what is needed in future years to make them able to cope with adversity. Your children need the knowledge to know that they will be fine in all life circumstances, no matter what their conditions are.

I encourage you to ask your children to practice visualizing themselves in a positive light, talking about themselves in a positive way, and cultivating this positive image of themselves. Try to do it too, as your child will learn this much faster if they see it in your behavior.

Sometimes it might be difficult for your or your child to visualize something in the future. So, ask them to close their eyes and see themselves doing the activities they really love or they would love to learn to do. For example, dancing on the stage, playing a guitar, playing football and scoring goals. Whatever it is that they really want to achieve, they need to be able to imagine it first. By doing so, they will be practicing the positive visualizations which will support them in building positive self-image and forming perfect basis for taking full responsibility for their lives.

2

INTRODUCE SELF-DISCIPLINE

Self-discipline is a very important aspect of building healthy self-esteem in our kids. People with low self-esteem often say *"I can't achieve my goals because I don't believe in myself."* It's worth pointing out that some kids might really need our help with believing in themselves but in some cases, this is just an excuse. It can be very easy to say, *"I don't believe in myself. I'm not going to be able to do it anyway, so what's the point trying."*

Self-discipline means being consistent in your actions. And here, parents have a real chance to shine and lead by example. So, what it means is that we need to think about how consistent we are in our daily life. Are we able to complete our tasks from start to finish? When we say we are going to do something, are we really doing it?

How do we model self-discipline to our children? As we know, kids learn from us whether we notice it or not, so how can we teach them determination and self-discipline? It's something that parents really must cultivate. One way of doing it is trusting yourself and demonstrating that you can count on yourself and commit to your tasks no matter how big or small they are. This is a crucial element to our and our kids' development. Kids with low self-esteem often agree to different tasks that they know deep inside they can't complete. They do that purely to get a compliment or approval from adults or other children. People with low self-esteem will look for an opportunity to get a compliment or an approval so they can feel better about themselves. Children with a healthy level of self-esteem know what they're capable of and they actually are very eager to impress us with their discipline. So, let's remember that seeking approval from others can often slow us down in completing important tasks and it's not something that our children should be thinking about or being focused on. What's important is to get to know themselves well enough, like themselves enough, and trust themselves enough to only say *YES* to the tasks they are able to complete. And in case they don't want to complete certain tasks, they have the ability and the skill to explain why this is something they can't complete.

Children with healthy self-esteem know themselves enough to know when they are not able to complete something. Promising others things we can't deliver on makes us feel very uncomfortable and gives us a real sense of disappointment, so it should be avoided as much as possible. Also, by agreeing things we can't deliver on we are also re-confirming our self-esteem. Children with healthy self-esteem have a level of self-control about them. They know what they are capable of. They don't easily give away control to other people and then they blame it on external conditions when something didn't work out. That is the skill that we, parents, really need to pay attention to. This is because we want to teach our children to be in control of what happens to them in their life in order to be in control of their actions and decisions instead of pushing responsibility on other people and blaming other people or external conditions that something didn't work out. I'm sure you have noticed people in your circle who have this real victim attitude. And they are always quick to blame that something didn't work out for them because of an external situation or other people. This is not something we should be practicing in our children.

There are many ways you can use to teach self-discipline to your children. One way of supporting your children's self-development is showing them how we are consistent and disciplined. How we, adults, live our life and what we do when we struggle. By sitting down with your children and looking at the tasks they need to complete, helping them to break them down, and really putting heads together and helping them in completing this goal, we can achieve a lot. So remember, the easiest and most effective way children learn is by observing us. By teaching them self-discipline, we are empowering them to make decisions on their own, what they want to focus on and why.

Self-discipline is like an internal muscle of your will. The more you use it, the stronger it gets.

<u>10</u>

IMPROVE THEIR FOCUS

When it comes to creating new healthy habits, staying focused is very important. There are many effective ways in which you, as a parent, can help your child improve their focus. For example:

Designate a distraction-free space for learning. So, the first condition is to assign space in the house that will be used for doing homework and sticking to this space. This is much better than randomly choosing a different place every day. So, carve out an area specifically for lessons and homework and stick to it.

Provide ventilation with a good light and reduce noise in this space. Look around your home and select a space that has good ventilation and a daylight reaching to it. This will help keep your child's mind staying focused and refreshed.

So select a place that is away from distractions and away from the noise and one that has a good light.

Remember to put extra gadgets away. Keep away any devices such as games consoles, TV, tablets, mobile phones during this time. The only gadget that a child should be using is a laptop or any other device used for taking lessons or doing homework. Once the homework is over, I recommend that you put the laptop away and you encourage your child to either write on a piece of paper with a pencil or go outside.

Keep topped up with water and snacks. Make sure your child has enough water, enough snacks, and enough nutrition while they are studying whether they are preparing for exams or just simply completing their homework.

Design visually appealing spaces. Many children get the motivation to do work in a well decorated space. Children like different colors, designs, and patterns. They generally do really well in a well-decorated space. Allow time to decorate their homework station with craft by seeking some help from children themselves. Your child will be excited to help you with this. Visual stimuli will make them want to come back to it every day. Also, put all the school supplies - their books, pens, and pencils - in a place easy for them to reach in a caddy.

Other things you can do to help improve your child's focus:

Set realistic goals

Do this together with your child. Ask them what their study goals are and what you can do to help them achieve it. Is there an exam approaching soon? If so, what's the date for it? Do they need a certain grade to get accepted to their favorite school or college? Have an honest chat about it.

Divide their work into segments

By helping them divide their homework into doable chunks, your child will not feel overwhelmed which could result in them losing interest and focus. So have a look at the whole content of their homework and see how you can best divide it into easier, smaller chunks.

Stay away from multitasking

Make sure your child studies one subject at the time. Multitasking could confuse them and overwhelm them, so try avoiding this if you can.

Make sure they take breaks

Take breaks between each subject. Perhaps you can ask your child to take a walk with the dog outside or go to the garden for 10 minutes to get some fresh air. This might help them to get a fresh perspective and keep them motivated.

Use motivating words

Do so especially while setting goals and working on them. Don't forget the power of constructive words. Make sure you use reassuring statements or something that makes a child excited about the homework such as:

- *It will be fun doing these things today, don't you think?*
- *I'm sure you will do so well with your assignments.*
- *We are going to finish everything together.*
- *What's your favorite subject? Let's do this first.*
- *How about making friends with mathematics today?*
- *How about inviting spellings to our notebook today?*

IMPROVE THEIR BODY POSTURE

We said earlier that a parent can be a really good teacher and an example for a child to follow. The way you talk and sit matters a lot whether a child is going to listen to you or not. You should have a relaxed but composed body posture that is not too casual. Having this posture will allow you to build rapport with your child and they will mirror it, too. Ask your child to sit properly with upright posture where their spine is straight and erect.

USE POSITIVE AFFIRMATIONS

A confident child always tries to complete a task on time. A child with low self-esteem might find it really hard to concentrate. There is a chance that they will be absorbed in a negative self-talk that will prevent them from getting involved in the present moment. They might look for excuses and blame external factors for their lack of motivation or a *"predicted"* failure instead of doing their best. You can use positive affirmations to boost learning in your child. Try using phrases such as:

- *You are such a smart child!*
- *Wow, that's an excellent answer - well done!*
- *You have done your homework really well today.*
- *Good job - high five! You are a shining star!*
- *Awesome! I love this essay you have just written.*
- *I love being around you.*
- *You will be great! I believe in you!*
- *I'm so proud of you!*
- *You are doing really well - keep it up!*

SUMMARY

Congratulations - you came to the end of this book. I hope you found the information included in this book helpful and perhaps you are already using some of them in your daily life with your child. There are a couple of things I want to mention before we officially say goodbye. One of them is that low self-esteem is not like having a cold. It doesn't just go away one day. It's something that it's built over the years and it takes practice to improve. It's great you've reached out for this resource. I hope that it will help you understand your child's perspective on things, see their point of view, create a bond with them, and improve your communication.

However, remember that you need to respect the fact that creating a positive self-image and self-esteem is as much your child's work as it is yours. And you can't do all the work for them. So depending on what your child's approach is to this - this will mean everything. You as a parent play your role in this process and your child plays their role.

Another thing I want to mention is that children observe us all the time. The easiest and fastest way for your children to build good confidence and a positive self-image is to model that from you - their parents. They see that in your behavior, in your words, and how you communicate with one another. They will simply store that in their mind as a behavioral model and learn from it. This is something I really want you to remember. So look at your own self-esteem and your self-image. Practice positive self-talk and do all the work needed to really cultivate this positive self-image in yourself. Your child will observe that and learn from that. You have the content of this book available indefinitely. I hope you find it useful.

Milton Keynes UK
Ingram Content Group UK Ltd.
UKHW021329280723
425958UK00015B/480

9 798223 444466